the korean people's democratic republic

Glenn D. Paige

Integration and Community Building Among
The Fourteen Communist Party-States

JAN F. TRISKA, ED.

the korean people's
democratic republic

Integration and Community Building Among
The Fourteen Communist Party-States

Jan F. Triska, Editor

Volume I

HOOVER INSTITUTION STUDIES: 11

the korean people's democratic republic

Glenn D. Paige

The Hoover Institution
on War, Revolution, and Peace
Stanford University, Stanford, California

The Hoover Institution on War, Revolution, and Peace, founded at Stanford University in 1919 by the late President Herbert Hoover, is a center for advanced study and research in public and international affairs in the twentieth century. The views expressed in its publications are entirely those of the authors and do not necessarily reflect the views of the Hoover Institution.

Copyright © 1966 by the Board of Trustees of the
Leland Stanford Junior University

Library of Congress Catalog Card Number: 65-27783
Printed in the United States of America

CONTENTS

PREFACE

This study of the Korean "People's Democratic Republic" is part of a symposium sponsored by the Stanford University Studies of the Communist System. The subject of the symposium—integration and community-building among the fourteen Communist party-states[1]—represents one of several conceptual, methodological, and research undertakings which this project supports and fosters.

Studies of the Communist System, inaugurated at Stanford in 1963 with the assistance of a five-year grant from the Ford Foundation, is part of the expansion of international studies throughout the University. The research here undertaken has been centered upon the world Communist movement as a system—its origins and development, its behavior and operations, its various subsystems and boundaries, the differential concepts of identification (and self-identification), and the severally perceived beliefs, preferences, and values of Communist elites as they affect the system's cohesion. To support and complement the emphasis on interactional and comparative models applicable to the system as a whole, specific systematic inquiries into the basic properties of individual units of the system and their contributions to the system's harmony or disharmony have been undertaken.

The principal assumption underlying the symposium is

7

that the Communist party-states have displayed, over time, certain objective properties and propensities that predispose them toward a greater or lesser degree of cohesion—cooperation, coordination, integration—with other party-states. We think that the present behavioral characteristics of the system can be traced to environmental, attitudinal, and systemic factors that generated or affected the origins, development, and operation of the member units, and that we can learn a great deal from a comparative description of the several stages in the process of integration into the system of the member units.

The focus of our research in the symposium is the process through which political units become part of a larger political entity. They do so by force or by consent; through similar or shared institutions as well as through similar codes of behavior; through integration at the elite level only or at lower levels as well, and so on. Major studies concerning the formation of larger political units in the West European, North Atlantic, East Asian, African and other settings have already been completed;[2] systematic treatment of the process of unit integration in the Communist party-state system, on the other hand, has been limited to parts of the system and usually covers a relative short time-span.[3] Hence, our symposium undertakes to study political "becoming" and integration into larger units over a long span of time.

The concept of political integration and community formation and maintenance is, as a focus of intellectual curiosity and investigation, as old as the study of politics. The mushrooming of supranational integrational movements since World War II has given a considerable new impetus to the old curiosity and has changed the emphasis of investigations. Social scientists who in the last two decades have been building a general theory of political integration, whether on a subnational, national, or supranational level, have been perhaps less concerned with the philosophical content of the concept of integration than with discovering operational indicators that would endow the concept with empirical meaning and would allow the theory to be tested for validity and reliability.[4] The principal centers of their inquiry have been two broad independent variables, *interaction* and *attitude*. Although in most cases investigated separately, interaction and attitude are assumed to combine to constitute a *community*, the *objective* of the *process* of integration.[5]

The principal subjects of inquiry have been *transactions across* the boundaries of units and *attitude formation* within the units. The theorists stipulate that substantial amounts of transactions are necessary for political integration and postulate that the densities of transactions among the units indicate their relationship. Flow of mail and telephone traffic; trade; aid; exchange of tourists, officials, and migrants; cultural exchange of persons and communications; newspapers, periodicals, and book sales and translations; radio, TV, and motion picture exchange; mutual treaties and agreements; and common organizations and conferences are the kinds of indicators that, measured and plotted over time, should demonstrate the direction of integrational trends and developments.

With reference to *attitude formation*, theorists have been more concerned with the process of integration than its *results* (conditions) within the units. The pertinent literature yields relatively little on this subject. In *Nationalism and Social Communication*, Karl Deutsch argues that it may be fruitful to study two sets of persons within a unit of analysis: those "mobilized" for integrational communications and those "assimilated" into the new, larger unit. If those assimilated multiply at a more rapid rate than those mobilized, then "assimilation" is gaining and "community is growing faster than society."[6]

9

Studies of the *results* of the integrational process, though more attractive as actual achievements of the integrational process, are more difficult to carry out. Attitude formation is still almost impossible to study in the Communist party-states because of the great sensitivity of the officials and decision-makers; relevant aggregate data are not easy to come by, and pertinent survey data are well-nigh unobtainable.[7] One of the most critical problems in the area of Communist studies has been the lack of an empirically testable theory. The data problem, though especially severe in the particular case of the Communist party-states, has hampered the building of general theory of political integration as well, and has made systematic comparative analysis very difficult. Lacking data, those who have been interested in the development of theoretical integrational constructs have had to rely on indicators of degrees and trends. Such indicators, although they offer valuable information, depend a great deal on inference.

How, then, do we engage in case studies prior to the day when adequate data will be available? In a word, we proceed by treating uneven data rigorously. First of all, the symposium relies on the expertise of the individual authors when describing such central attitudinal issues as basic and goal values and their distribution; expectation of goal achievement; cultural orientation; and compatibility of demands relevant to integration. By cross-referencing these issues against the party-state's socioeconomic system, its historical development and ecological-physical factors, as well as against such data as are available, we hope that the symposium, though imperfect, will offer conclusions that will contribute to the construction of interim, low-level theory of political integration and community-building among the Communist party-states.

Each study in the symposium follows a common outline

composed of five major headings. These five principal sections represent specific, significant developmental periods in the integrational process of the party-states: (I) *The pre-entry period* contains an analytical description of the party-states before they became party-states. This section, like those that follow, however, is limited to what the individual authors believe to be essential to the party-state's becoming a unit within the party-state system. Thus, the section attempts to identify, analyze, and evaluate the phenomena relevant to the unit's future integration. As a consequence, each state's ecological-physical factors, its demographic structure, its belief system, its social system, and its degree of autonomy from and dependence upon other states are examined against the background of hopes, expectations, and needs within the state for integration with other states and systems.

The pre-entry period is followed by four other key historical developmental periods differentiated in terms of the effects that these developments have on the integration of the party-state into the system: (II) *The entry of the party-state into the Communist party-state system,* (III) *Stalinism,* (IV) *the Thaw,* and (V) *the present stage.* Within these broad confines, the individual contributors use the same conceptual scheme as in the pre-entry period; but each devotes more space to those periods of the outline in which important changes took place and which are more significant, in their view, for the integrational development of the party-state in question.

The overall conceptual design stipulates variables at a relatively high level of generality for two reasons: first, because the individual case studies represent a chiefly exploratory research operation, and second, because the common design was constructed to guide the original research, not to bind it. The differences among the individual party-

11

states are such that a set of predetermined, rigid prescriptions would harm, rather than foster, the theoretically relevant comparisons we wish to make.

Because of the overall focus of the symposium, on the other hand, the case studies contain empirical analyses of only those party-state phenomena, factors, and variables that are *system-relevant*, that is, which contribute to integration or conflict with other party-states. The symposium is not planned to be yet another collection of writings about Communist countries; instead, it is a collective study of that behavior of the individual party-states which is *system-relevant*. It is not a series of descriptive case studies of the party-state but a collective system-approach study of data relevant for *integration* and *conflict* of the party-states. In other words, only system-relevant information is of interest to us. This approach in turn calls for a scheme of categories cutting across the conventional legal-political categories of traditional comparative studies: we wish to bring *system-relevant social characteristics* of the individual party-states into clear focus.

We assume that the degree of integration and community can be measured only in relative terms: the amount of cooperative achievement in one sector of endeavor can be compared with the amount of cooperative achievement in another sector. We further assume that there are several kinds of integration among the party-states: (1) In terms of *units*, integration may oscillate from integration of elites only to party-state-wide integration, and from practices only (no integration of units) to complete institutional unification. (2) In terms of *method*, integration may be the result of force, at one extreme, or of consensus, at the other. (3) In terms of *benefit-cost* analysis, integration may vary from extremely costly to highly economical. In addition, we assume that *compatibility* of institutions, practices, and values should be differentiated from *similarity* among institutions, practices, and values. Whether *similarity* may or may not foster integration depends on the *compatibility* of integrational objectives.

Finally, the symposium is based on the assumption that the Communist party-states, shaking themselves free from obsolete Stalinist ideas and methods of organization, do not reject the need for association as such. For Communist parties that have already captured power, the idea of a world Communist community united in opposing capitalism and imperialism and carrying out a historical destiny is real and necessary. To do anything that might precipitate an irrevocable, final schism is, we think, instinctively repugnant to all Communists as splitting their world-wide movement at a critical time.

The symposium is an intellectual product of many creative minds. In addition to the authors of the specific studies, I would like to single out for particular acknowledgment of their original contribution and assistance from among the staff of the Stanford Studies of the Communist System the following individuals: David D. Finley, James S. Morrison, John E. Rue, and Bruce Sievers. Peter J. Duignan, the Executive Secretary of the Hoover Institution, originally suggested this series and, together with Hoover's Curator of East European Collections and Director of Publications, Karol Maichel, was instrumental in bringing about its publication.

JAN F. TRISKA

Institute of Political Studies
Stanford University
February 10, 1965

13

INTRODUCTION

> Without doubt there is a revival
> of nationalism. . . . Economic
> progress does not dispel this, it
> nurtures it.
>
> PALMIRO TOGLIATTI, 1964[1]

If integration is conceived of as "an index of cooperative action produced by coordination of behavior and unified institutions," and is taken to vary in terms of "units, methods, and benefit-costs," then gross changes in North Korea's integration within the Communist system during the period from 1945 to 1964 might be summarized in the following manner. In terms of *units,* the external-integration pattern of North Korea has changed from one of a high degree of integration with Imperial Japan, to virtually exclusive integration with the Soviet Union, and finally to a more varied pattern of integration with states within and outside of the Communist system. In terms of *methods,* North Korea's mode of integration has changed from being highly submissive to Japanese and Stalinist assertiveness to relying upon bargaining techniques. In terms of *benefit-costs,* the psychological costs of subordination in an assertive pattern of integration with one or more party-states of the Communist system have become increasingly intolerable, despite such benefits as flow from this kind of integration. Thus North Korean Communist leaders increasingly have tended to reject transnational integration of institutions at all levels and are tending to avoid situations in which other party-states might exercise a veto power over their decisions. In general, during the course of nearly twenty years, North Korea seems to have moved toward a pattern of integration within the Communist system that increasingly resembles the traditional alliance pattern of states in the European nation-state system.

The immediate historical background of the above changes provides a general explanation for them: North Korea entered the Communist system directly after it had been integrated within the Japanese Empire and did so precisely at a moment when long-smouldering Korean aspirations for autonomous and independent development were high. North Korea became a Communist party-state against the background of the main thrust of modern Korean political history: the steady growth of Korean nationalism.[2]

Taking the above-mentioned changes in North Korea's integration within the Communist system as descriptive of the main dependent variables to be explained, and taking Korean colonial experience as the basis from which change took place, the first chapter will examine North Korean developments over the past twenty years. The examination will seek for insight into the processes by which change occurred. Later North Korea's pre-entry position, Stalinist integration, and post-Stalinist integrative change will be examined. In conclusion, some projections of past trends into the near future will be suggested.

16

1

THE PRE-ENTRY PERIOD

Korea has three major neighboring nations, which are the objects of its potential international integration: China to the north and west, Russia to the north, and Japan to the east. At present, the North Korean capital of Pyongyang is situated approximately 500 air miles from Peking; 3,200 air miles from Moscow, or 425 miles from Vladivostok; and about 875 miles from Tokyo. North Korea shares a northern border of over 800 miles with China and of 11 miles with the Soviet Union. By sea the North Korean port of Chongjin is only about 580 miles from the Japanese port of Niigata. These geographical proximities have conditioned the human geography that has become a part of North Korean awareness of the external environment. At present over one million Koreans live in China (mainly in the Yenpien autonomous Korean *chou*, just north of the Yalu River frontier);[1] about 300,000 live in the Soviet Union (principally in Central Asia, where they were moved by the Soviet Government from the Maritime Provinces during 1935–37); and over half a million Koreans live in Japan (many of whom were originally recruited as laborers during the period of Japanese rule). On the other hand, there are no sizable national minorities in Korea, not even Chinese. In the more immediate external environment, of course, are the more than 26 million Koreans who live south

17

of the Thirty-eighth Parallel in the Republic of Korea. About 11 million Koreans live in North Korea itself.

The modern history of Korea, from its opening to international trade in 1876 to 1945, can be seen in part as a contention between, on the one hand, internal or external forces conducive to integration with either China, Russia, or Japan and, on the other, those forces inhibiting such integration in favor of increased Korean autonomy. After half a millennium of deferential autonomy as a tributary state of the Chinese Empire,[2] Korea was first removed from the traditional Chinese international system by Japan as a result of the Sino-Japanese War of 1894–95, then secured against the threat of predominant Russian influence in the Russo-Japanese War of 1904–5, and finally placed under direct Japanese colonial rule in 1910. As a small but growing people, numbering about 13.3 million in 1910[3] and about 25 million in 1945, living on a peninsula of 220,768 square kilometers, and surrounded by giant nations, Koreans view their modern history as a tragic international drama in which they have been the victims of great power rivalry.

In 1945 the Red Army entered Korea, the only underdeveloped former colonial country opened to it by the fortunes and misfortunes of World War II. Korea had just undergone thirty-five years of alien rule and was well advanced toward integration within the Japanese Empire under the wartime slogan "Japan and Korea One Body" (*Naisen ittai*).

Politically, administratively, and militarily, Japanese exercised direct control over the Korean people. Koreans were exhorted and, insofar as possible, compelled to carry out the responsibilities of citizens of Japan. Japanese held a large majority of key positions in the administrative bureaucracy, the police, the military, industry, and education. For example, 86 percent of 4,652 higher officials in 1943

18

were Japanese. Of 87 occupants of the strategic posts of bureau chiefs in the central bureaucracy from 1910 to 1943, only two were Koreans.[4] Authoritative decisions were made for Korea by the Imperial Japanese Government and by the Government-General of Korea. The conduct of Korean foreign relations was entirely in the hands of the Japanese Foreign Ministry.

Korean participation in decision-making, limited to a small portion of the Korean elite, was largely consultative and advisory. A kind of privy council of notables to advise the governor-general was established in 1910. After the mass protest demonstrations of 1919, the Japanese established a system of semi-elected advisory councils at the district (*myon*), municipal (*pu*), and provincial (*to*) levels. At least half of the council memberships tended to be Japanese residents of Korea. Voting was limited to males with certain age and tax qualifications. A belated Japanese plan of January 1, 1945, to secure the election of 10 Korean representatives to the upper house of the Diet and 16 Korean representatives to the lower house was never carried out.[5] There were no legal Korean political parties. The domestic Korean Communist movement was fragmented and underground. Despite continuing attempts to rebuild a viable Communist Party after its suppression by the Japanese police during 1925–28 and its expulsion from the Communist International in 1928, the party could not be reorganized.[6] Subjected to effective police repression at home, small scattered groups of Korean Communist revolutionaries agitated abroad: some joined the Chinese Communist Party or followed Mao Tse-tung to Yenan; others formed separate armed guerrilla bands based on the Korean population in Manchuria; still others carried their hopes for Korean revolution and independence to the Soviet Union, although Soviet authorities apparently did not encourage the activities of Korean revolutionary organizations on Soviet territory. Other Koreans nurtured their clandestine communism in Japan.

The nationalist movement for Korean independence demonstrated somewhat more continuity than the Communist movement, but it was largely ineffective against the Japanese inside Korea. The main symbol of Korean independence was the emigré Korean Provisional Government that had been organized in Shanghai in 1919 and had since carried on a tenuous existence in the shadow of the Kuomintang. It sought support from other nations, including the United States, but met with little success. During the war years, the Provisional Government followed the Chinese National Government to Chungking in order to recruit Koreans in China to fight the Japanese.

However much the Korean nationalist and Communist revolutionaries may have differed on other matters, they were agreed on at least one thing: Korea must be freed from Japanese rule. They were agreed also on the unlikelihood that Korean independence could be gained by the efforts of the Korean people alone; it would have to be gained through international collaboration. While the Communists looked primarily to the Soviet Union for assistance, the nationalists looked primarily to America, Europe, and China. Within Korea there had been only one mass protest against Japanese rule: the nationwide street demonstration of March 1, 1919. The demonstration had begun peacefully and had then been crushed by violent Japanese police and military action. Since then, the Korean people as a whole had acquiesced silently to the fact of Japanese power. They were disappointed in the lack of international interest in their plight, but they still looked for allies who might help in breaking Japanese rule.

Economically, the Koreans viewed their country as the victim of exploitation in the interests of Japan.[7] The Koreans, who had only a handful of modern industries in

1910, viewed the Japanese buildup of mining, metallurgical, hydroelectric power, transportation, and other facilities in northern Korea not as an attempt to further Korean interests, but simply as an attempt to assure Japanese industries of raw materials and to support Japanese military and industrial operations in Manchuria. The Koreans also resented the way the Japanese exploited southern Korean agriculture so that they could export large amounts of rice each year. Korea was then primarily an agricultural country, with 70 percent of the population engaged in farming. Like Korean diplomatic relations, Korean international trade relations were under direct Japanese control.

Culturally, Koreans viewed themselves as the objects of Japanese efforts to force them to assimilate. Although the institutions of the Yi dynasty from 1392 to 1910 had been patterned on the Chinese model, and although Koreans were highly conscious of a wide range of cultural borrowings from China, especially in social relations and government, Koreans also jealously guarded their sense of cultural distinctiveness.[8] In the first stages of colonial rule the Japanese seem to have emulated Tsarist methods of subjugating minority peoples[9] and relied on rather crude techniques for asserting Japanese cultural as well as political authority; for example, Japanese teachers wore swords, presumably to instill proper fear and respect in their pupils. After the uprising of 1919 the Japanese learned to employ more subtle methods, but the crude assertion of superior power was never really abandoned—for the Japanese found themselves faced by a proud and culturally homogeneous people.

A principal tactic of cultural assimilation employed by the Japanese was the gradual displacement of the Korean language by Japanese. Japanese was the official language of administration and education. While structurally similar to Japanese, and while having many Chinese borrowings,

21

the Korean language was a distinctive one. Although there were some regional dialectical variations, all Koreans were intelligible to one another, and could not be understood by either Chinese or Japanese. Koreans were proud of their simple alphabetic system of writing, *Hangul*, invented in the mid-fifteenth century. In modern times this system permitted them to dispense with the use of Chinese characters if they wished. The Korean language was a prized symbol of national identity.

After 35 years of colonial rule, the Japanese had made substantial progress in linguistic assimilation of the Korean elite, but this was only a small fraction of the population as a whole. In 1942, only about 20 percent of 25 million Koreans were classified as "competent in Japanese."[10] On the other hand, about 70 percent were regarded as "illiterate," apparently meaning lacking ability to read either Japanese or Korean. The immediate reason the Japanese language failed to become widely used by the bulk of the Korean population was, of course, the very limited Japanese investment in Korean education. In 1945, only about 8 percent of Koreans were attending school: 1,163,-042 in primary school, 249,584 in middle school, and 29,439 in high school or college.[11] Only one Korean in a thousand was being educated beyond the middle-school level, where a high degree of competence in Japanese was required. Japanese professors and students dominated Keijo Imperial University in Seoul, the principal institution of higher learning in Korea. The Japanese-educated Korean elite occupied minor but crucial positions in the bureaucracy, the police, the military, industry, education, and in other areas; they were needed to link the rulers and the ruled.

The mass-communications pattern in Korea in 1945 reflected the way that the Japanese controlled the elite politically and attempted to assimilate them culturally. The largest Japanese newspaper was the *Keijo-Nippo* (Seoul News), with a circulation of 375,000.[12] In addition, Japanese-language newspapers were published in each of Korea's thirteen provinces. Only one Korean-language newspaper was published, the *Maeil Sinbo*, organ of the Japanese Government-General of Korea, which reached a circulation of 500,000. Two independent Korean-language dailies had been suppressed in 1940: the *Tong-A Ilbo* (Orient Daily News) and the *Choson Ilbo* (Korea Daily News), with circulations of 55,000 and 63,000 respectively.

Thus when Japan acknowledged defeat in the Pacific war on August 15, 1945, Korea was highly integrated with the Japanese home islands politically and economically, but was less well integrated socially and culturally. Having lost their political and economic integrity, Koreans clung desperately to their language and culture for a sense of national identity.

The arrival of—first Soviet, then American—occupying forces in August and September of 1945 brought an end to Japanese control and permitted the expression of political aspirations by newly formed political groups. The long-suppressed Korean desire for independence was emphatically proclaimed, especially in Seoul, where most of the Korean political elite was active. "We seek the construction of a completely independent state," declared the Preparatory Committee for National Revival, a coalition group to which the collapsing Japanese administration had hoped to transfer responsibility for maintenance of social order.[13] "We seek the attainment of an autonomous, independent state for the Korean nation" (*minjok*), affirmed the Korean Democratic Party.[14] The newly revived Korean Communist Party in Seoul promised, "We shall struggle to the end for

23

the complete liberation of the Korean nation, for the elimination of the remnants of feudalism, and for democratic free development."[15]

In the early party pronouncements of the post-liberation period, there were also statements that could be interpreted as evidences of a recognition of the necessity or desirability of international cooperation as a means of achieving Korea's objectives. Six sociopolitical organizations in Seoul issued a joint statement in which they promised to become "the most responsible proponents of international cooperation."[16] The Korean Democratic Party, in a statement implying a need for other nations to respect Korean pride and independence, called for "diplomatic relations based on mutual respect and equality." This party also declared its intention to work for world peace by "adherence to the United Nations Charter" and through "sincerity, righteousness, and love."[17] The Korean Communist Party in the United States Military Government zone proclaimed, "Hail the Soviet Union! Hail the Chinese Communist Party!"[18] The reference to the Chinese Communists was unusual, for North Korea had fallen under control of the Stalinist Red Army, and early public announcements of the Korean Communist Party that was being formed in Pyongyang under its aegis apparently made no mention of the Chinese Communist movement.

2

THE ENTRY OF NORTH KOREA INTO THE COMMUNIST PARTY-STATE SYSTEM

Both the Japanese system of colonial integration and Korean national unity were broken by the Soviet-American division of Korea into two parts after August 15, 1945. The North Korean Communist party-state emerged formally out of three years of Red Army occupation with the proclamation of the Democratic People's Republic of Korea (DPRK) on September 9, 1948. By 1950 there was some evidence to suggest that North Korea was "already well advanced toward becoming a republic of the USSR."[1] Thus in the short period of five years the northern part of Korea had shifted its pattern of integration from Japan toward the Soviet Union.

The forced termination of the integrative relationship with Japan and the gradual hardening of the Thirty-eighth Parallel as a virtually impenetrable internal frontier caused great dislocations in North Korean political, economic, and social life. North Koreans numbering about 8.5 million found themselves cut off from about 16.5 million fellow countrymen in the South. Instead of being inhabitants of a country of 220,792 square kilometers with a population density of 117 persons per square kilometer, they found themselves artificially restricted to an area of 127,135 square kilometers with a population density of 69 persons per square kilometer. There were no major linguistic, religious, or ethnic differences between the people of North and South; a culturally homogeneous people simply had been divided into two unequal groups. This was important for North Korea's international integration, since it has meant that North Korea since 1945 has faced an attractive but as yet non-Communist object of integration in the South.

Since Korean public administration was centralized in nature, the division of the country was especially disruptive. All of the ministries and their controlling bureaus were located in Seoul, now cut off from the North Korean city of Pyongyang, which had become the center of governmental activities in the North. Under both the Japanese and the traditional Korean administrative systems, the provincial authorities had little real policy initiative and were not coordinated laterally.

The dislocations caused by the severance of the lines of authority centered in Seoul were compounded by the hasty departure of thousands of Japanese officials. According to South Korean figures, at least 705,239 Japanese civilians left Korea in the period after liberation.[2] Many of these must have fled from North Korea in the path of the advancing Red Army or shortly thereafter. Among those who departed were administrators, policemen, and teachers, as well as industrial managers and technicians.

Economic disruptions in 1945 were heightened both by the departure of Japanese managers, technicians, and skilled laborers and by the severance of relations with Japan and the South. The Russians and the Korean Communists, as the immediate heirs of Japan's industrial legacy in Korea, found themselves in possession of the facilities to produce 80 percent of Korea's coal, 95 percent of its iron and steel, 90 percent of its hydroelectric power, and 85 percent of its chemicals.[3] Thus the chemical, metallurgical, and power industries of the North were cut off from the textile, machine-building, and consumer goods industries of the South. The heavy industries and their raw material base in the North were divorced from light industrial and agricultural complements in the South. North Korea in 1945 accounted for only about 33 percent of Korea's food production and only about 20 percent of its consumer goods output. Agriculturally, partition left North Korea with one-third of the rice-paddy land and two-thirds of the dry-field farming area.[4]

The forced termination of integrative relationships with Japan and the political-geographic division of the country set the conditions under which the early integration of North Korea into the Communist system took place. These conditions were far from those of autonomy and independence that Korean revolutionaries had envisioned. North Korea was still dependent; it was occupied by the Red Army; it lacked an acceptable Korean political authority; its centralized administrative system was disrupted; it was short of food and consumer goods; and its economy was distorted by paralyzed, skill-deficient industries.

The Soviet military presence was the best guarantee that North Korean political development would be in the direction of Communist integration. But there was a political tension from the very start between those who aspired to autonomy for Korea and those who favored closer collaboration with the Soviet Union. Some sensitivity to such aspirations can be seen in the first public statement of the Soviet military commander, General Chistiakov, in 1945:

Korea has become a free state, but this is only the first page in the history of New Korea. Just as a flourishing garden is the result of human effort and care, so also the happiness of Korea can be achieved only through the efforts and steadfast struggle of the Korean people.

Citizens of Korea! Remember that happiness is in your own hands: you have received freedom and independence; you must

27

maintain that freedom and independence by all means. The Soviet Army has provided all the conditions for the free creative work of the Korean people. The Korean people themselves must become the creators of their own happiness.[5]

The same appreciation of the potency of Korean aspiration for national independence is revealed in the first public statement in Korea of Kim Ilsong. A 33-year-old native Korean with both Manchurian and Soviet experience, he was to become with Soviet support both premier of the DPRK and chairman of the Korean Workers Party after 1948. Kim was introduced as a partisan hero at the Pyongyang mass meeting of October 14, 1945. It was apparently he who struck the following note of fervent national aspiration at the meeting:

We sincerely thank the Soviet Army which has fought for our freedom and liberation. Japanese imperialism, which had oppressed us for thirty-six years, has been smashed by the heroic campaigns of the Soviet Army. After thirty-six years of darkness our nation has emerged into the light; having received liberation and freedom, it shines brightly with hope that pours over the mountains and rivers of our land like the morning sun.

The Korean nation must go forth from this time, uniting its forces in the construction of a new democratic Korea. No party, faction, or individual can complete this great task alone. Let all who really love their country and freedom join together in complete, national, harmonious solidarity to create a democratic, autonomous, independent state—the rich, with their money; the learned, with their knowledge; the workers, with their labor.[6]

Although there is as yet no detailed study of Soviet policy in Korea in 1945–46, both the Chistiakov and Kim statements need to be interpreted within the context of contemporary events. The Soviet forces, which entered Korea three weeks before American forces, had first penetrated south of the Thirty-eighth Parallel and had then withdrawn. In December 1945, just four months after Chistiakov's and Kim's statements, the Soviet Union advocated a four-power trusteeship for a united Korea. Thus there appeared

28

to be some initial hesitancy in Soviet determination to incorporate Korea within the Soviet system.

While the presence of the Red Army guaranteed a Soviet veto over Korean decisions, the Russians, in filling the political-administrative vacuum left by the departing Japanese, chose to exercise indirect rather than direct control. This was in contrast to direct United States military government in South Korea from 1945 to 1948. The basic Russian strategy was to place native Koreans—some rather inept, but all undoubtedly responsive to Communist direction—in positions of the highest formal authority, and to place Soviet-Koreans[7] or Russian advisers in locations of de facto power. A prime example of the workings of the Russian strategy was the case of Kim Ilsong himself; he became first secretary of the North Korean Communist Party in October of 1945, while the Soviet-Korean Ho Kai, a member of the CPSU, took the powerful Stalinist post of head of the party organizational bureau.

There were two main sources of Communist opposition to the Kim-Soviet alliance in the years immediately after liberation: the Yenan-Koreans and the domestic Korean Communists. Presumably the former might have been expected to favor integration with China; the latter could have been expected to be more resistant either to Russian or to Chinese integration. The Kim-Soviet alliance was relatively but not unchallengeably dominant in the years from 1945 to 1948. A Yenan-Korean, Kim Tubong, became chairman of the North Korean Workers Party (NKWP) when it was formed as the result of a merger of his New People's Party with the North Korean Communist Party in 1946. Kim Ilsong served as vice-chairman. He emerged as chairman only in 1948, when the NKWP and the South Korean Workers Party, headed by Pak Honyong, joined in a single Korean Workers Party (KWP). The factional balance of power at the highest levels is illustrated by the triumvirate of top leaders that emerged: Kim Ilsong as chairman, Kim Tubong (Yenan-Korean) and Pak Honyong (South Korean) as vice-chairmen. Opposed to all three of these men were nationalist leaders scattered in the underground or in jails, some of whom were assassinated as time went on; these nationalist leaders feared both domestic communization and international absorption by the USSR, and commanded considerable popular sympathy. The strength of the political attitudes these leaders espoused seems to explain in large part the emphasis given to Korean independence and class harmony in the early Christiakov and Kim statements. It also helps to explain why an incumbent Communist leadership would wish to ally closely with Soviet power in order to maintain its supremacy over Korean alternatives.

Soviet-American negotiations about Korean trusteeship broke down during 1945 and 1946; the Korean question was shifted to the United Nations in 1947, and the Republic of Korea was established on August 15, 1948. During the course of these events the Russian and Korean Communists gradually shaped the North Korean Communist party-state that emerged formally as the DPRK on September 9, 1948. This was preceded by the formal organization of the Korean People's Army in emulation of the Red Army on February 8, 1948.

Economically the establishment of the DPRK was preceded by land reform on a private ownership basis in March and April of 1946, the nationalization of 90 percent of major industries in August of 1946,[8] and the one-year plan of 1947 and 1948. Until 1953 the North Koreans refrained from the collectivization of agriculture and the complete elimination of private economic activity. They probably refrained because the Pyongyang leaders hoped to be able to entice the people of South Korea into integrating with them, not because they had any insuperable problems

30

in establishing political control in the North. The political line of the pre-1950 period was "Create a democratic revolutionary base," not "Build socialism."

The economic rehabilitation of North Korea involved the reorientation of the Korean economy from Japan to the Soviet Union. At first, idle industries were nursed into operation with the help of Red Army technicians; specialists appeared later, until almost every major North Korean industry had its Russian adviser. Gradually the ferrous and nonferrous metal industries, the chemical, the cement, and the power industries were revived. The output of valuable industrial raw materials, 80 percent of which had previously been exported to Japan in an unprocessed state,[9] was directed toward the Soviet Union, which became North Korea's leading trading partner. Trade with the Soviet Union in 1950 was planned to be more than three-quarters of North Korea's total foreign trade. One-third of this trade was in military goods, and there are indications that the North Koreans were required to pay for most if not all of their Soviet military supplies.

Although the extent and nature of Soviet-Korean economic relations were a closely guarded secret in the pre-1950 period of North Korea's entry into the Communist system, documents captured in the Korean War have permitted some insight into the degree of economic integration that took place. They reveal the Soviet Union's primary interest in North Korean iron and steel, minerals and metals. This is illustrated by Table 1, which gives production and export plans for 1950.

Major Korean imports were crude oil, coal, chemicals, machinery, spare parts, and railroad equipment. Close supervision was exercised over Korean gold production, with nine tons of refined gold planned for export to the USSR in 1950. North Korea was required to pay for the services of Soviet technicians after 1949 and possibly be-

TABLE 1

Allocations of North Korean Production to Soviet Union, 1950

(1,000 metric tons)

Item	Planned Production	Planned Export to USSR
Nonferrous metals		
Copper	2,915.0	400.0
Lead	12,405.0	8,000.0
Zinc	19,450.0	10,000.0
Tungsten	2,900.0	1,350.0
Iron and Steel		
Iron Ore	910.0	50.0
Pig Iron	370.0	100.0
Special Steel	16.5	12.8
"Common" Steel	169.2	49.5
Chemicals		
Fertilizer	416.0	90.0
Carbide	143.0	40.0

Source: Dept. of State, *North Korea*, p. 109.

fore. A Soviet loan of 212 million rubles was to be supplied during 1949 and 1951; grants were apparently not made. These decisions were made or acceded to by the Soviet-Koreans who held important posts in Korean foreign-trade agencies.

On the basis of these and other data, State Department analysts of the Research Mission dispatched to North Korea in October 1950 concluded that "the economy of North Korea, to an ever-increasing degree, was being integrated into the Soviet economic orbit." Prophetically, writing in 1951, these same analysts anticipated the demands for economic balance and independence that were to be raised with increasing insistence by the Korean Communists in the following decade. "The expansion of heavy industry in North Korea," the American investigators wrote, "appears to have been directed toward meeting Soviet requirements and in the long run to have conflicted with what would appear to be legitimate North Korean interests in developing a more nearly balanced and self-sufficient economy."[10]

During 1945–50 Japanese cultural influence was displaced, "advanced Soviet culture" was introduced, and the sense of Korean cultural identity revived. The symbol of the Korean national renaissance under Communist direction was the restoration of Korean as the official national language and the abolition of Chinese characters in the mass media. This took place in June 1949. Furthermore, North Korean enthusiasm for education opened an avenue for the importation of Russian science, technology, language, literature, art, and other subjects, and of political indoctrination as well. In 1944 North Korea was instructing only 35 percent of its primary-age schoolchildren and had only 50 middle schools (with but 1.8 percent of the total number of students), three technical schools, and no colleges.[11] By 1948 it was claimed that adult illiteracy had been eliminated and that there were 5,000 middle schools, 69 technical schools, and 15 colleges.[12] But these claims were probably exaggerated, and Korea was undoubtedly still dependent in terms of technical skills. It was estimated that about 500 Koreans were studying in the USSR in 1949.[13] According to the Soviet-Korean cultural agreement of 1949, about 150 Koreans a year were to be sent to the USSR for study.

For some Koreans the Communist emphases on the study of the Russian language was reminiscent of Japanese cultural imperialism. By 1948 the study of Russian had been made compulsory at the middle-school level; later, instruction began in the fifth grade. Top-level officials in the bureaucracy were expected to be fluent in Russian, and there was a rigorous effort to promote the study of the language among leaders throughout the country.

Other Russian cultural influences were to be seen in translations, art, dance, the theater, movies, press, and radio. The Russian military and political presence, the ascendancy of the Korean Communists, the shattering of Japanese cultural domination, and the growth of Korean educational aspirations were accompanied by the importation and widespread emulation of Russian cultural models. Even after the rise of the Chinese Communists to power in 1949, there was no comparable rise in Chinese cultural influence in North Korea before the Korean War.

Thus by June of 1950 a Soviet-controlled leadership had established its organized rule over North Korea; an army had been created that was advised, trained, and equipped by the USSR and staffed by Soviet-Koreans; the Korean economy had been revived and reoriented from integration with Japan toward integration with Russia; and Russian cultural influence was increasing in proportion to the output of a rapidly expanding educational system. Non-Communist Korean nationalists were bitterly castigating the Kim Ilsong faction as "traitors" and "Russian puppets." It is not likely that the sting of nationalist taunts was lessened by the hard choices that the Pyongyang leadership must have had to make as North Korea under Russian tutelage was progressively integrated into the Stalinist system.

3

INTEGRATIVE AND NATIONALIST IMPLICATIONS
OF THE KOREAN WAR, 1950–53

The war experience of 1950–53 merits special attention in assessing the integrative potentials of the North Korean party-state. When the details of the decision to attack the Republic of Korea are revealed—as perhaps they will be in the course of Sino-Soviet polemics—they should greatly aid in the analysis of North Korea's position within the Communist system, both then and now. What seems clear already is that the North Koreans could not have invaded the South without Russian foreknowledge and approval, if not initiative. The extent of Chinese involvement in the original decision is problematical.[1] The assumption of Soviet foreknowledge is based partly upon several revealing facts. First, there was a tight network of Russian advisers and Soviet-Korean officers that stretched from the Defense Ministry in Pyongyang to at least the division level of the Korean People's Army. Second, during April and May 1950 the Soviet Union provided North Korea with heavy artillery, tanks, and airplanes far superior to those available to the Southern forces. Finally, Soviet authorities maintained close control over the Korean People's Army through monthly allocations of vital petroleum products.[2] And, on the other side, it is certain that the war did not result from South Korean initiative, however much the idea of the forceful unification of Korea might have appealed to President Rhee.

Internationally, the war diversified Korean involvement in the Communist system and intensified Korean demands upon that system. With the failure of the initial offensive because of the American and United Nations intervention, more than a million Chinese fighting men entered North Korea, and Russia lost its unique position as the only important Communist ally of North Korea. After this point a Soviet–Chinese–North Korean Joint Military Council apparently coordinated the efforts of the Chinese military units and the Russian military advisers.[3] The Supreme North Korean directorate for the prosecution of the war was a seven-member Military Affairs Committee, headed by Kim Ilsong. Conflicts must have arisen within and between these decision-making groups about the conduct of the war. Despite the general goodwill that seems to have existed between the Chinese troops and the Korean populace, there is some evidence that professional North Korean officers sometimes resented being placed under Chinese command.[4]

North Korean demands on the Communist system must have been intense in late September and October of 1950, when South Korean and United Nations forces were rolling northward, eventually occupying most of the DPRK. It is undoubtedly of great significance that at this moment of crisis, when a few days would have meant the extinction of the North Korean party-state, the crucial aid came from the Chinese—not from the Russians. Although the Russians provided advice, fighter pilots, weapons and other military supplies, and relief goods, the Pyongyang leadership apparently was not content; they wanted infantry divisions equipped with heavy support weapons, and they wanted the Russians to mount an air bombardment against the Republic of Korea.[5]

Although the evidence is fragmentary, a reasonable hypothesis seems to be that neither the inception nor the subsequent prosecution of the Korean War caused the North Koreans to be more satisfied with their collaboration with the Soviet Union. Indeed, the North Koreans must have been greatly relieved when the Chinese decided to intervene, even though Sino-Korean relations during and after the war must have involved some friction.

The war seems to have resulted in the strengthening of domestic Communist control in North Korea, especially of the position of the Kim Ilsong faction. The wartime chaos permitted the Communist regime to murder many of its opponents; many others fled to South Korea. Although the Korean Communist Party was on the verge of disintegration in October 1950, when about 80 percent of KWP members "lost" their party identification cards, it was able to revive, although it needed the presence of the Chinese and Soviet support to do so. This revived party restored public administration, maintained a minimum level of economic production, and kept a fighting army in the field.

Partly by accident, perhaps, the Kim Ilsong leadership, during and immediately after the war, was able to eliminate some key alternative leaders whose ascension to power might have led to closer relations with China or the Soviet Union or to a more independent Korea. Thus the purposes of the Kim Ilsong leadership were served by the purge of the Yenan-Korean General Mu Chong, the suicide of the Soviet-Korean Ho Kai, and the execution of the South Korean Pak Honyong, who seems to have been killed as a scapegoat for the failure of the war. Kim Ilsong leaders, whose ascendancy dates from 1945, survived the turbulence of the war and maintain their positions at the present time. This means that whatever integrative changes have occurred have been correlated with changes in the factional composition of the central decision-making group, but not in the dominant faction: Kim and the Kapsan group. In other words, policies have changed, but not the leaders primarily responsible for making those policies.

The wartime experience undoubtedly led to a reinforcement of Korean nationalistic aspirations. Appeals to Korean nationalism coupled with attempts to teach the virtues of proletarian internationalism had been prominent themes in Korean Communist and Soviet propaganda of the prewar period. Undoubtedly the existence of a non-Communist Korea on the southern flank of the DPRK justified the nationalist emphasis. However, the nationalist appeals of Kim Ilsong were unconvincing to most Koreans. For example, although the Communist leader referred to the concept of *minjok* ("nation," with ethnic implications) 46 times in his Liberation Day address of August 15, 1946, he made 65 references to the Soviet Union or to the Red Army in the same speech.

The war did not immediately displace the Soviet Union as Korea's ostensible "benefactor" and as the powerful "leader of the socialist camp," but it did lead to a new Korean self-image. In a speech Kim Ilsong delivered on July 28, 1953, in which he dealt with the recent truce, he extolled "the fatherland—for our people this is the most precious [thing]."[6] The war had been labeled from the start as the Fatherland Liberation War. The Korean Communists now portrayed themselves as victors over modern American military technology, as heroic defenders of the "eastern outpost of the socialist camp," and as thwarters of American plans to turn North Korea into a military base from which to assault China and the Soviet Union. Never before in all history, it was incessantly proclaimed, had the Korean people faced such an evil and powerful foe; never before had they demonstrated such heroic patriotism and unity in resistance.

Economically, the effect of the war was to leave North

TABLE 2

EFFECT OF WAR ON NORTH KOREAN PRODUCTION, 1949
COMPARED WITH 1953

Type of Production	1949	1953
Electric power (million kwh)	5,924	1,017
Coal (metric tons)	4,000,000	708,000
Steel ingots (m. tons)	144,403	3,610
Cement (m. tons)	536,614	26,513
Chemical fertilizer (m. tons)	401,157	negligible

Source: *Development of the National Economy and Culture of the People's Democratic Republic of Korea (1946–1959)*, JPRS: 4148, 31 October 1960, pp. 30–31.

Korea crippled and deeply dependent upon the Communist system for aid in reconstruction. Gross industrial production in 1953 was said to be 36 percent of that in 1949. Some indicators of the economic setbacks brought by the war are given in Table 2.

In 1953, North Koreans needed food, clothing, medicines, building materials—virtually everything required to make life bearable.

Thus when North Korea entered the war in 1950 it could expect increasing political, economic, and cultural integration with the USSR. It left the war in 1953 still a viable party-state, primarily oriented toward the Soviet Union but also open to more varied integrative relationships with other Communist countries, especially China. In addition, the war had stimulated North Korean nationalist sentiments but had left the country economically more dependent on bloc support than it was before the war.

4

INTENSIVE SOCIALIST DEVELOPMENT OF NORTH KOREA, 1953–64

The intensive socialist development of the North Korean Communist party-state has taken place in three stages in the postwar decade since the death of Stalin: a three-year plan for postwar economic reconstruction, 1954–56; a five-year plan of industrial development, 1957–61; and the current seven-year plan of industrial consolidation and expansion, 1961–67. The postwar decade began with North Korea in a position of extreme economic dependence upon the Soviet Union and the other states of the Communist system; it ended with North Korea in a position of substantial economic independence. The war began with North Korea in a position of virtually unquestioned subservience to political direction by the Soviet Union; recently we have had North Korean declarations of "complete agreement" with Chinese Communist contradictions of Soviet policy views and multiplying signs of North Korean political independence. Since the North Korean economic development in the postwar decade was correlated with the emergence of a substantial degree of political deviation, it is tempting to view the former as the "cause" of the latter. But the Korean case suggests that it is more accurate to view the two elements as forming a mutually influencing relationship and to relate them to other domestic and international changes that took place in the ten years after the truce. That is, the economic development that perhaps facilitated resistance to external political direction was itself partly brought about by political decisions motivated by desires for greater autonomy. Economically, North Korea has achieved both growth and balance in the postwar decade. Both were initially made possible by the provision of substantial postwar aid by the USSR, China, and the other states of the Communist system and by joint decisions between the North Korean and other Communist leaders about how aid should be used. Certainly there must have been inter-party conflicts over the amount and kind of aid, as there was within the KWP itself.

In the postwar decade the Soviet Union provided at least two billion rubles in grants and credits,[1] the services of 1,500 technicians, and advice, technical documentation and equipment for some 40 industrial enterprises. Among Soviet-aided projects have been the Pyongyang textile combine, the Hungnam chemical combine, the Supung hydroelectric station, the Kim Chaek metallurgical plant, the Takchong automobile plant, the Sariwon tractor-repair plant, the Madong cement plant, the Yongsong meat combine, and the Sinpo fish cannery.

In 1964, the Soviet Union was aiding in the construction of an electric power plant with an atomic reactor, evidently a prestige project for political effect in view of North Korea's vast hydroelectric resources. It had also agreed, sometime during 1959–61, to build an oil refinery with an annual capacity of two million metric tons and to provide by 1967 the crude oil essential for its use. Since North Korea is critically dependent upon foreign oil, and since North Korea's only refinery, located at Wonsan and run formerly as a joint Soviet-Korean stock company, was destroyed in the war, the Soviet agreement to build and supply raw material for an oil refinery appears to have been both a belated concession to Korean needs and an attempt to maintain a vital economic link.[2]

Chinese contributions of grants and credits to North Korea were estimated at 1.8 billion rubles in 1961.[3] Chinese assistance began with cancellation of all wartime debts and the provision of 325 million dollars in goods that included railroad rolling stock and building materials.[4] On September 28, 1958, at a time when the North Koreans were experimenting with the communes of the Chinese type, China loaned Korea 10 million dollars to help build the Unbong hydroelectric station on the Yalu River. At the same time an additional credit of 42.5 million dollars was extended for additional projects, including the Sinuiju textile mill (North Korea's second largest), and the Hwoeryong sugar factory. On October 13, 1960, at a time of increasing Sino-Soviet tension, the Chinese Communists made their largest postwar loan—105 million dollars for the period 1961–64—in order to assist the North Koreans to develop radio-communication facilities and to set up plants for the manufacture of rubber tires and machines.

In addition to Soviet and Chinese assistance, North Korea received, according to a Japanese source, more than 600 million rubles in grants from other countries of the Communist system for immediate postwar reconstruction. (The distribution of these grants is shown in Table 3.) In addition, Mongolia supplied some 17,000 horses.

In the early postwar period this aid brought a diversification of North Korean relationships within the Communist system. Czechoslovakia has aided the reconstruction of hydroelectric power plants, the construction of one of Asia's largest machine-tool plants, and a nonferrous-metal rolling shop. Rumania has contributed a metallurgical plant, a steel tubing shop, and an aspirin plant. Hungary has aided the construction of a machine tool plant, a chem-

TABLE 3

GRANTS TO NORTH KOREA FOR POSTWAR RECONSTRUCTION
FROM COMMUNIST STATES

Country	Million Rubles
East Germany	217.0
Poland	164.4
Czechoslovakia	113.0
Rumania	90.0
Bulgaria	20.0
Hungary	15.7
Total	620.1

Source: *Asahi*, July 14, 1961, p. 3.

ical dye plant, and a plastics plant. Poland has built railway repair shops at Pyongyang and Wonsan.

Despite protests within the KWP, the Kim Ilsong leadership emphasized the development of heavy industry during the three-year plan of 1954–56, and in the first five-year plan, although concessions were made at the behest of critics to the goal of economic balance: the "simultaneous development of light industry and agriculture" was promised. The gains achieved by emphasis on rebuilding and expanding heavy industry are suggested below.

In 1958 North Korea produced, according to Soviet technical documentation, its first trucks and tractors, its first metal trawler (a ship of 450 tons displacement), and its first electric locomotive. During 1963, North Korea was reported to have produced 3,033 tractors and 4,022 trucks.[5] "At present," the leading Soviet writer on the contemporary North Korean economy explained in 1963, "Korea has its own machine-tool, automobile, tractor, and shipbuilding industries and has established plants that produce mining, chemical, metallurgical, and agricultural equipment and parts."[6] By 1960, as a further indicator of

TABLE 4

PRODUCTION IN NORTH KOREAN HEAVY INDUSTRIES, 1944–63

Type of Production	1944	1953	1956	1963
Power (million kwh)	813	1,017	5,120	11,766
Coal				
(thousand metric tons)	5,740	708	3,908	14,040
Steel ingots (m. tons)	146,569	3,610	189,943	1,167,000
Rolled steel (m. tons)	105,247	3,512	132,701	870,000
Cement (m. tons)	893,596	26,513	597,015	2,780,000
Chemical fertilizers				
(m. tons)	511,740	—	195,063	950,000

Source: *Development of the National Economy and Culture of the People's Democratic Republic of Korea (1946–1959)*, JPRS: 4148, October 31, 1960; Korean Central News Agency release, January 17, 1964.

growing self-sufficiency, it was reported that about 90 percent of all machinery and equipment used in North Korean plants had been produced by Koreans.

The plans for industrialization after the war also aimed at balancing and diversifying North Korean industry; it was to include industries such as textiles that had been cut off in South Korea. Textile production increased from 1.4 million meters in 1944 to 21.6 in 1953, 77 in 1956, and 227 in 1963.[7]

As industry developed in the postwar decade, its contribution to gross economic output came to surpass that of agriculture. North Koreans now thought of their country as primary industrial rather than agricultural. The contribution of industry changed from 42.4 percent of gross value of economic output in 1953 to 70 percent in 1961. At the same time the proportion of the population classified as "workers and office employees" grew from 29.7 percent in 1953 to 52 percent in 1960.[8]

The growth of industry in the postwar decade contributed to the declining dependence upon foreign aid, the diversification of the international trade patterns within and

TABLE 5

Sources of State Receipts,
North Korea, 1956–60
(percentage figures)

State Receipts	1956	1958	1960
Socialist sector	74.6	93.5	95.3
Taxes	8.8	2.8	2.1
Foreign grants and credits	16.6	3.7	2.6

Source: Kim Samgyu, *Chosen no shinjitsu* (The Truth about Korea—Tokyo: Shiseido, 1960), pp. 74, 91.

without the bloc, and the decreasing reliance upon foreign technicians or the training of Koreans abroad. By 1957 at least 7,763 students and technicians had returned from study abroad. In 1959 the number of Korean students sent overseas was "drastically reduced."[9] The decline in foreign aid is shown in Table 5.

Changes in North Korea's trade pattern showing the declining Soviet predominance, the rising importance of trade with Communist China, and the small but growing trade with non-Communist countries are presented in Table 6. While no current figures are available, there is no reason to believe that these trends have changed. Since 1960,

TABLE 6

AREAS OF NORTH KOREAN FOREIGN TRADE, 1955–57
(percent of total trade)

Trading Partners	1955	1956	1957
Soviet Union	80.8	75.0	57.0
Communist China	9.0	10.3	27.3
Other Communist countries	10.0	14.4	12.6
Non-Communist countries	.2	.3	3.1

Source: Yoon T. Kuark, "A Comparative Study of Economic Development Between North and South Korea During the Post-War Period," MS, University of Minnesota, 1961, p. 27.

North Korea has been importing grain from Australia. Since 1961, a vast increase in trade with Japan has occurred, with North Koreans exporting Musan iron ore for the Japanese steel industry. In addition, the North Koreans have recently attempted to expand trade with such "nonaligned" countries as Indonesia, Guinea, and Egypt.[10]

Social changes in the postwar decade have included a declining farm population, a growth of the industrial and clerical labor force and consequent urbanization, and a steady rise in the North Korean educational level with special emphasis on technical training. For example, in 1961, 65 percent of 97,000 students in 78 North Korean colleges specialized in engineering or in other technical fields. Table 7 shows the effort being made to develop the skills required for industrial life.

TABLE 7

STUDENT POPULATION AND SCHOOLS, NORTH KOREA,
1953–54 AND 1959–60

	1953–54	1959–60
Number of students	1,776,000	2,526,000
Number of schools	4,606	8,300

Source: Song Chihak, *Chosen kyoiku-shi* (History of Korean Education—Tokyo: Kuroshiyo, 1960), p. 210.

The figures for 1960 indicate that 25 percent of a population of approximately 10,030,000 growing at a rate of 2.8 percent per year[11] were attending school.

One of North Korea's most striking socioeconomic changes in the postwar period is the complete collectivization of agriculture that took place in the short period from 1953 to 1958. In the same period the elimination of all private ownership in industry and trade was also completed. The relative ease with which agriculture was col-

46

lectivized in North Korea may be explained partly by the presence until late 1958 of the Chinese People's Liberation Army. While it has often been claimed that collectivization, mechanization, electrification, and chemical fertilizers have made North Korea self-sufficient in food grains, in recent years the country has steadily imported grain from abroad, especially from outside the Communist system.[12] Food-grain needs, which will rise with the growth of population, can be expected to increase North Korea's dependency upon the outside world.

Politically the postwar decade has seen a growth in KWP membership, unsuccessful factional struggles to oust the Kim Ilsong leadership, and resistance to interference by other Communist parties. The party grew from 360,000 members in 1946 to 750,000 in 1948, and on to 1,160,-000 in 1956 and 1,310,000 in 1961. The KWP thus encompasses about 12 percent of the North Korean population. Its unusual size is defended on grounds that it is needed for the task of national unification.

Factional struggles in the postwar period have involved both domestic issues and party relations within the Communist system. The elimination of a domestic opposition in the period from 1953 to 1955, after an attempted coup, was justified largely on the grounds that the opponents were "hired agents of American imperialism." Actually, it seems likely that one of the issues underlying the conflict was agricultural collectivization.

Within the KWP in August 1956, soon after the Twentieth CPSU Congress, the Soviet-Korean and Yenan-Korean Communists attacked the Kim Ilsong leadership for its "personality cult," its emphasis upon heavy industry to the neglect of popular needs, and on other issues.[13] Since the influential Soviet-Korean leader Pak Changok seems to have written a letter of complaint to Khrushchev about Kim Ilsong at this time, and since Kim successfully weathered the subsequent attempt to oust him from the KWP leadership, it is likely that this is one of the grievances against Khrushchev that by 1964 had brought the KWP to denounce the intervention of "certain persons" in the internal affairs of small countries in the "socialist camp." There was a conspicuous departure of Russians (except for technicians and military advisers) and Soviet-Koreans from North Korea after 1956.[14] The purge of the Yenan-Koreans involved in the 1956 opposition continued over the next two years. It reached its climax with the purge of Yenan-Korean army officers that followed an abortive coup planned by Lieutenant General Chang Pyongsan for May 1, 1958.[15]

Hence the Fourth Congress of the KWP in September 1961 was hailed as the "congress of victors." Kim Ilsong claimed that factionalism had been completely eradicated from the Korean Communist movement. In retrospect, it seems that the Kim Ilsong group first relied upon external support (the Red Army and the Soviet-Korean and Yenan-Korean returnees), to gain control of North Korea in 1945–48; it then relied upon a combination of external and internal factors (the Chinese military, the overseas returnees, and wartime grievances) to eliminate in 1953–55 the potential national Communist opposition of the South Korean Labor Party group. Gradually the group took advantage of nationalist sentiments and in 1956–58 eliminated the Soviet-Korean and Yenan-Korean influences. Finally the group emerged in 1961 as the leaders of Korean Communism, championing the "purity" of Marxism-Leninism against "modern revisionist" despoliation, and lauding "self-reliance" as the supreme national virtue.

Kim Ilsong seems to have displayed remarkable skill in balancing contending forces, in the timely alteration of factional alliances, and in appreciating within limits the strength of Korean needs for respect and independence that have grown throughout the last century. One might predict that Kim's eventual successor will be someone even more dedicated to basic Korean needs rather than an advocate of closer integration into the Communist system or systems.

The Kim Ilsong leadership entered the postwar decade apparently still responsive to Soviet policy direction. At the end of the decade it was emphatically rejecting Soviet leadership on a wide range of policy issues (including the proposal to convene an international congress of Communist parties in 1964) and was suggesting that the political conflict among the national Communist parties had become so severe that it threatened to disrupt normal "state relationships." Attacking by name "the CPSU leadership," the Korean Communists in August 1964 decisively rejected any kind of hierarchical authority pattern in the international Communist movement. "All fraternal parties are *equal* and *independent*," they declared. "There may be a large party and a small party but not a higher party and a lower party, nor a guided party and a guiding party." One sentence amounted virtually to the end of the idea of involuntary political integration with the Soviet Union, or by implication, eventually with Communist China: "No majority principle or no centralized discipline is applicable to the relations among fraternal parties."[16] If there was to be no authority structure in party relationships, could there be one in state, economic, military, and cultural relationships? Since the party is conceived as directing all other relationships, the answer is clearly no.

5

EVALUATION, TRENDS, AND PROSPECTS

In 1945 the predominant political aspiration in Korea was for national independence. The desire for independence was frustrated by integration with the Soviet Union, but Chinese wartime intervention initiated a weakening of the Soviet integrative pattern. Postwar economic development was accompanied by growing emphasis on Korean self-reliance; that growing self-emphasis was correlated with greater diversification of relationships both within and without the Communist system, and the KWP leadership finally emerged openly, at least by 1962–64, as a Chinese ally on a wide range of issues involved in the Sino-Soviet dispute.

A major factor for the changes that have taken place has been the influence of modern nationalism: a widespread desire to reject foreign interference in Korean affairs, to revive Korean cultural pride, and to receive international respect. The influence of nationalism undoubtedly has been increased by the unprecedented involvement of the population in political organization. It is important to note, however, that the kind of nationalism permitted in North Korea does not challenge the basic premises of North Korea as a Communist party-state. It emphasizes the autonomy and self-reliance of such a state and rejects the idea of political or economic subordination in a Communist international system. Korean Communist nationalism has thus far displayed a narrow range of creativity; non-Communist nationalism has not yet played a major role in North Korea.

North Korea's emergence from integration in the Communist system has, of course, resulted from changes in the external environment itself. Ideological emphasis on Korean autonomy in Kim Ilsong's ideological writings came in 1955,[1] two years after the death of Stalin. Overt deviation from Soviet policy direction was possible only with Chinese protection. Thus North Korean policy changes have been a product of the interaction between internal needs and external opportunities.

Looking toward future prospects for integration within the Communist party-state system, it is to be noted that North Korea must import oil, coking coal, rubber, and food grains (estimated at 5 to 10 percent of consumption requirements). With a population increasing at about 2.6 percent per year and an expanding industrial plant, these needs may be expected to grow year by year. There is little indication, however, that these needs can or must be satisfied fully within the present Communist system; thus the North Koreans can be expected to diversify their economic and political involvements with nations outside the system.

An alternative Korea and American power in the South introduce extremely complex considerations into any prediction. In general, however, it might be said that the less integrated North Korea appears to be within the Communist party-state system, the greater its attraction as an object of integration to the people of South Korea. On the other hand, the less integrated with or the more alienated from the Communist system or systems the North Korean party-state becomes, the greater the probability of its transformation and absorption within the larger Korean polity.

At the same time, fear of the power of the American-supported Republic of Korea means dependence on Communist political and military alliances. The contemporary willingness of the KWP leadership to risk serious conflict with the CPSU leadership, however, probably means that the ROK-American threat is not viewed in Pyongyang as so serious that it cannot be met mainly, if not exclusively, with Chinese support. As long as a Communist party-state remains viable in North Korea, as long as a viable non-Communist alternative remains in the South, and as long as the antagonisms that sparked the Korean War endure, any Communist leadership group in Pyongyang can be expected to maintain at least the minimum integrative relationships within an international Communist system or subsystem that will ensure its survival. For example, despite their political deviation from the Soviet line, the North Koreans apparently have maintained military and technical assistance relationships with the Russians. But the greater the self-confidence in their own ability to attract, infiltrate, and seize control of the Republic of Korea, the less will be their reliance upon international integrative relationships. In short, the North Korean Communist party-state has moved in the direction of the international relations that have characterized the Western nation-state system.

NOTES

Preface

1. By "Communist party-states" we mean the fourteen states
ruled by the Communist parties, or, as *Pravda* (February 10,
1963, p. 2) puts it, where the Communist parties are "at the
helm," namely, the USSR, the People's Republic of China, the
People's Republic of Albania, the People's Republic of Bulgaria,
the Hungarian People's Republic, the Democratic Republic of
Vietnam, the German Democratic Republic, the Korean People's
Republic, the "Heroic People of Cuba," the Mongolian People's
Republic, the Czechoslovak Socialist Republic, the Polish People's Republic, the Rumanian People's Republic, and the Socialist Federal Republic of Yugoslavia. Both the Communist Party
of the Soviet Union and the Chinese Communist Party recognize
Cuba as one of the Communist party-states; China excludes Yugoslavia.

2. Ernst B. Haas, *The Uniting of Europe* (Stanford: Stanford
University Press, 1958); "International Integration," *Interna-
tional Organization*, XV (1961). F. Gunther Eyck, *The Benelux
Countries: An Historical Survey* (Princeton: Princeton Univer-
sity Press, 1959). Frantz Wendt, *The Nordic Council and Co-
operation in Scandinavia* (Copenhagen: Munksgaard, 1959).
Norman J. Paddelford, "Cooperation in the Central American
Region," *International Organization*, XI (Winter 1957). David
Apter, *The Political Kingdom in Uganda* (Princeton: Princeton
University Press, 1961). James S. Coleman, *Nigeria: Back-
ground to Nationalism* (Los Angeles: University of California
Press, 1958). Lucian Pye, *Politics, Personality and Nation Build-
ing* (New Haven: Yale University Press, 1962). Bruce M. Rus-
sett, *Community and Contention: Britain and America in the
Twentieth Century* (Cambridge: The MIT Press, 1963).

3. George Modelski, *The Communist International System*
(Research Monograph No. 9; Princeton University: Woodrow
Wilson School of Public and International Affairs, 1960),

p. 9. Zbigniew Brzezinski, "The Organization of the Communist Camp," *World Politics*, XIII, no. 12 (1961) ; "Peaceful Engagement in Communist Disunity," *China Quarterly*, no. 10 (April-June 1962). Kurt London, "The Socialist Commonwealth: Pattern for Communist World Organization," *Orbis*, III, no. 4 (1960). Paul Shoup, "Communism, Nationalism and the Growth of the Communist Community of Nations After World War II," *American Political Science Review*, LVI, no. 4 (December 1962). Jan F. Triska, "Conflict and Integration in the Communist Bloc," *The Journal of Conflict Resolution*, V, no. 4 (1961). Richard Lowenthal, *World Communism: The Disintegration of a Secular Faith* (New York: Oxford University Press, 1964). Kazimierz Grzybowski, *The Socialist Commonwealth of Nations: Organizations and Institutions* (New Haven: Yale University Press, 1964).

4. Leonard Binder, "National Integration and Political Development," *American Political Science Review*, LVIII, no. 3 (September 1964). Karl W. Deutsch, *Nationalism and Social Communication* (New York: Wiley, 1953) ; *The Nerves of Government* (New York: The Free Press of Glencoe, 1963) ; "The Growth of Nations: Some Recurrent Patterns of Political and Social Integration," *World Politics*, V, no. 2 (January 1953) ; "Social Mobilization and Political Development," *American Political Science Review*, LV, no. 3 (September 1961). Deutsch *et al.*, *Political Community in the North Atlantic Area* (Princeton: Princeton University Press, 1957) ; Deutsch and Louis J. Edinger, *Germany Rejoins the Powers* (Stanford: Stanford University Press, 1959) ; Deutsch and William J. Falts, eds., *Nation-Building* (New York: Vinton Press, 1963) ; Deutsch and Richard I. Savage, "A Statistical Model of the Gross Analysis of Transaction Flows," *Econometrica*, XXVIII, no. 2 (July 1960). Amitai Etzioni, "The Dialectics of Supra-National Unification," *American Political Science Review*, LVI, no. 4 (December 1962) ; "A Paradigm for the Study of Political Unification," *World Politics*, XV (October 1962), pp. 44–74. Leonard W. Doob, *Patriotism and Nationalism: Their Psychological Foundation* (New Haven: Yale University Press, 1964). Rupert Emerson, *From Empire to Nation* (Cambridge: Harvard University Press, 1960). Philip E. Jacob and James V. Toscano, eds., *The Integration of Political Communities* (New York: Lippincott, 1964). George Liska, *Europe Ascendant: The International Politics of Unification* (Baltimore: Johns Hopkins Press, 1964). See also Talcott Parsons, *The Social System* (Glencoe: The Free Press, 1951), pp. 21 and 36, and Robert K. Merton, *Social Theory and Social Structure* (rev. ed.; Glencoe: The Free Press, 1957), p. 23.

5. Cf. Philip Jacob and Henry Teune, "The Integrative Pro-

cess: Guidelines for Analysis of the Bases of Political Community," in Jacob and Toscano. Or, as Ernst B. Haas (*Beyond the Nation-State: Functional and International Organization* [Stanford: Stanford University Press, 1964], p. 26) puts it, citing Paul Meadows ("Models, Systems and Science," *American Sociological Review*, XXII [1957], p. 6), "mutually supporting inputs into a social system tend to be associated with growth of structure, expansion of functions, development equilibrium—in short, a process summed up as 'integration.' " (Our own operational definition of integration is exclusively that of *conditions*, i.e., the index of results [effects, products] of cooperative action [joint action taken toward a common goal] produced by coordination [sharing of information in order to facilitate achievement of a common goal] of behavior and [unified] institutions.) See also Werner S. Landecker, "Integration and Group Structure: An Area for Research," *Social Forces*, XXX (1952), p. 395.

6. Deutsch, *Nationalism and Social Communication*, p. 99. See also Landecker.

7. For comparison see Ralph K. White, "Social Science Research in the Soviet Bloc," *Public Opinion Quarterly*, XXVIII, no. 1 (Spring 1964). K. Yu, "How the Soviet Institute of Public Opinon Conducted Three Polls," *Joint Publications Research Service* (U.S. Publ.), December 18, 1961. A. M. Gendin, "Communist Attitude Towards Work, Trends in Development," USSR Study, *Joint Publications Research Service* (U.S. Publ.), June 28, 1963. A. G. Kharchev, "Problems of the Family and Their Study in the USSR," *International Social Science Journal*, XIV, no. 3 (1962), pp. 539–49. Andrzej Sicinski, "Public Opinion Surveys in Poland," *International Social Science Journal*, XV, no. 1 (1963), pp. 91–110. J. Piotrowski, "Attitudes Towards Work by Women," *International Social Science Journal*, XIV, no. 1 (1962), pp. 80–91.

Introduction

1. *New York Times*, September 5, 1964, p. 2.

2. For an excellent survey from 1876 to 1945 see Chong-Sik Lee, *The Politics of Korean Nationalism* (Berkeley: University of California Press, 1963).

1—The Pre-entry Period

1. For a recent report on the Koreans in this area by a sympathetic Japanese visitor see H. Ando, "Enhen Kiko" (A Trip to

Yen Pien Korean Autonomous Region in People's China), *Toyo bunka* (Oriental Culture), no. 36 (June 1964), pp. 21–70.

2. For Korea's position see M. Frederick Nelson, *Korea and the Old Order in Eastern Asia* (Baton Rouge: Louisiana State University Press, 1946).

3. An important discussion of conflicting population estimates of Korea in the late 19th century is presented in a recent Soviet edition of an important Tsarist survey of Korea: I. S. Kazakevich *et al.*, *Opisanie Korei* (Description of Korea—Moscow: State Publishing House for Asian Literature, 1960), p. 333.

4. Pak Munok, *Hanguk Chongbu ron* (Korean Government—Seoul: Pomyongsa, 1963), p. 258.

5. Pak Munok, pp. 243–45, 251–53.

6. Glenn D. Paige, "Korea and the Comintern, 1919–1935," *Bulletin of the Korean Research Center*, no. 13 (December 1960), pp. 1–25.

7. Japanese control of the Korean economy is described in Andrew J. Grajdanev, *Modern Korea* (New York: John Day, 1944).

8. Cornelius G. Osgood, *The Koreans and Their Culture* (New York: Ronald Press Company, 1951).

9. Chong-Sik Lee, in *The Politics of Korean Nationalism* (Berkeley: University of California Press, 1963), p. 90, comments as follows: "The principal aide to Governor-General Terauchi up to 1914 was Lieutenant General Akashi Motojiro, who had studied the colonial policies of Russia while he was military attaché in St. Petersburg between 1902 and 1904. Terauchi, an Army general and Minister of the Army at the time of his appointment to the governor-generalship, was no expert in colonial administration. It is reasonable to assume that Akashi played a major role in shaping his policies in Korea."

10. Pak Munok, p. 288.

11. *Choson haebang illyon sa* (First Year History of Korean Liberation—Seoul: Munyu insogwan, 1946), pp. 347–48.

12. Ch'oe Chun, *Hanguk sinmun sa* (Korean Newspaper History—Seoul: Ilchogak, 1960), p. 31.

13. Yoronsa, *Chosonui changnaerul kyoljong hanun kak chongdang kak danch'e haesol* (Interpretations of the Various Political Parties and Social Organizations That Will Determine the Future of Our Country—Seoul: Yoronsa, 1945), p. 4.

14. *Ibid.*, p. 11.

15. Kim Chongbom and Kim Tongun, *Haebang chonhuui Choson chinsang* (The Actual Situation of Korea Before and After Emancipation—Seoul: Choson chongkyong yongusa, 1945), p. 62.

16. Yoronsa, p. 18.

17. *Ibid.*, p. 11.
18. Kim Chongbom and Kim Tongun, p. 63.

2—The Entry of North Korea into the Communist Party-State System

1. U.S. Department of State, *North Korea: A Case Study in the Techniques of Takeover* (Washington: U.S. Government Printing Office, 1961), p. 120.
2. *Kyongje yongam—1949* (Economic Yearbook–1949—Seoul: Research Section, Bank of Korea, 1949), p. 159.
3. Edwin W. Pauley, *Report on Japanese Assets in Soviet-Occupied Korea to the President of the United States* (Washington: U.S. Government Printing Office, 1946), p. 3.
4. Shannon McCune, "Korea: Geographic Parallels, 1950–60," *Journal of Geography*, LIX (May 1960), p. 204.
5. N. K. Vaintsvaig and V. V. Lezin, *Koreiskaya Narodnaya Demokraticheskaya Respublika* (Moscow: Academy of Sciences of the USSR, 1964), pp. 212–13.
6. *Choson chungang yongam 1949* (Korean Central Yearbook 1949—Pyongyang: Korean Central News Agency, n.d.), p. 63.
7. Estimates of the number of Korean residents of the USSR who returned to North Korea after 1945 have ranged from ten to thirty thousand.
8. Since 96 percent of industrial capital was owned by Japanese, this involved the disappropriation or alienation of only a few of the former Korean elite.
9. L. N. Karshinov, "Sotsialisticheskaya industrializatsiya v KNDR" (Socialist Industrialization in the DPRK), in V. S. Mirnov, ed., *15 Let osvobozhdeniya Korei* (Moscow: Institute of International Relations, 1960), p. 56.
10. Dept. of State, p. 109.
11. Song Chihak, *Chosen kyoiku-shi* (History of Korean Education—Tokyo: Kuroshiyo, 1960), p. 168.
12. *Ibid.*, p. 199.
13. Dept. of State, p. 111.

3—Integrative and Nationalist Implications of the Korean War, 1950–53

1. Allen S. Whiting, *China Crosses the Yalu* (New York: Macmillan, 1960).
2. Dept. of State, pp. 113 f.
3. Kiwon Chung, "The North Korean People's Army and the Party," *China Quarterly*, no. 14 (April-June 1963), p. 109.

4. Glenn D. Paige and Dong Jun Lee, "The Post-War Politics of Korean Communism," *The China Quarterly*, no. 14 (April-June 1963), p. 19.

5. *Ibid.*

6. *Wei cheng-ch'u tzu-yu tu-li ti Ch'ao-hsien jen-min cheng-i ti tsu-kuo chieh-fang chan-cheng* (The Korean People's Righteous Fatherland Liberation War for Freedom and Independence— Pyongyang: Korean Workers Party Press, 1955), p. 285.

4—Intensive Socialist Development of North Korea, 1953–64

1. *Far Eastern Economic Review Yearbook, 1962*, p. 149.

2. In view of the above-mentioned aid, Soviet anguish over the irony of the Peking-sponsored Second Economic Seminar of Asian Countries held in Pyongyang in the summer of 1964 can be appreciated. The seminar stressed "self-reliance" in the economic advance of the less-developed countries. Criticizing the conference theme, *Pravda* pointed out almost incredulously that conference participants had been taken to see the Pyongyang textile and Hungnam chemical combines, which were among those built with Soviet aid and technical assistance. *Pravda*, August 18, 1964, p. 3.

3. *Far Eastern Economic Review Yearbook, 1962*, p. 149.

4. The following details on Chinese Communist aid are from Ryozo Kurai, "Present Status of Japan–Communist China Relations," *The Japan Annual of International Affairs*, no. 1 (1961), p. 150.

5. Korean Central News Agency, January 17, 1964.

6. Karshinov, p. 66.

7. JPRS, 4148.

8. Chong-sik Lee, "Land Reform, Collectivization and the Peasants in North Korea," *The China Quarterly*, no. 4 (April-June 1963), p. 75.

9. Key P. Yang and Chang Boh Chee, "North Korean Educational System: 1945 to Present," *The China Quarterly*, no. 14 (April-June 1963), p. 133.

10. Thomas P. Thornton, "Foreign Relations of the Asian Communist Satellites," *Pacific Affairs*, XXXV (Winter 1962–63), pp. 341–52.

11. *Nicho boeki* (Japanese-Korean Trade), no. 39 (April 1962), p. 13.

12. No figures are available on total grain imports. In 1956, however, it was reported that North Korea imported 200,000 metric tons. A. I. Denisov, *Zarubezhnye strany* (Foreign Lands— Moscow: State Publishing House for Political Literature, 1957), p. 446.

13. The fullest account is given in Kim Changsun, *Pukhan siponyon sa* (Fifteen Year History of North Korea—Seoul: Chimungak, 1960), pp. 150 ff.

14. Glenn D. Paige and Dong Jun Lee, p. 23.

15. Kiwon Chung, p. 122.

16. North Korean radio broadcast, August 31, 1964; emphasis supplied. The contemporary level of tension is suggested by the perfunctory exchange of telegrams between the Soviet and North Korean foreign ministers and the subdued character of the embassy receptions that marked the sixteenth anniversary of the DPRK on September 9, 1964.

5—Evaluation, Trends, and Prospects

1. Kim Ilsong, "Sasang sopeso kyojojuui wa hyongsikjuuirul t'oejihago church'erul hwangniphal te taehayo" (On Exterminating Dogmatism and Formalism and Establishing Independence in Ideological Work), *Kim Ilsong sonjip* (Selected Works of Kim Ilsong—Pyongyang: Korean Workers Party Press, 1960), IV, 325–54.

FOR FURTHER READING

Early History

Kim, San, and Wales, Nym. *Song of Ariran*. New York: John Day, 1941.

Kuusinen, Otto. "O koreiskom kommunisticheskom dvizhenii" (On the Korean Communist Movement), *Revolyutionnyi vostok*, XI–XII (1931), 99–116.

Lee, Chong-Sik. "Korean Communists and Yenan," *China Quarterly* (January-March 1962), pp. 182–92.

———. *The Politics of Korean Nationalism*. Berkeley: University of California Press, 1963.

Paige, Glenn D. "Korea and the Comintern, 1919–1935," *Bulletin of the Korean Research Center*, no. 13 (December 1960), pp. 1–25.

Scalapino, Robert A., and Lee, Chong-Sik. "The Origins of the Korean Communist Movement," *Journal of Asian Studies*, XX (November 1960), 9–31; XX (February 1961), 149–67.

Post-1945

Bradbury, John. "Sino-Soviet Competition in North Korea," *China Quarterly* (April-June 1961), pp. 15–28.

Kim, Changsun. *Pukhan siponyon sa* (Fifteen Year History of North Korea). Seoul: Chimungak, 1960.

Kim, Ilpyong J. "North Korea's Fourth Party Congress," *Pacific Affairs*, XXXV (Spring 1962), 37–50.

Lee, Chong-Sik. "The 'Socialist Revolution' in the North Korean Countryside," *Asian Survey*, II.

Lee, Dong Jun. *Hwansanggwa hyonsil: naui kongsanjuui kwan* (Fantasy and Fact: My Observations of Communism). Seoul: Tongbang t'ongsin sa, 1961.

Paige, Glenn D. "North Korea and the Emulation of Russian and Chinese Behavior," in A. Doak Barnett, ed., *Communist Strategies in Asia*. New York: Frederick A. Praeger, 1963.

———. "Korea," in Cyril E. Black and Thomas P. Thornton, eds., *Communism and Revolution*. Princeton: Princeton University Press, 1964.

Rudolph, Philip. "North Korea and the Path to Socialism," *Pacific Affairs*, XXXII (June 1959), 131–43.

———. *North Korea's Political and Economic Structure*. New York: Institute of Pacific Relations, 1959.

Scalapino, Robert A., ed. *North Korea Today*. New York: Frederick A. Praeger, 1963.

Hoover Institution Studies Series

1. *The United States and the African Slave Trade 1619–1862,* by Peter Duignan and Clarence Clendenen. 1963. 72 p. $1.50.

2. *Communist China: The Politics of Student Opposition,* translated, with an introduction, by Dennis J. Doolin. 1964. 70 p. $1.50.

3. *Revolution and the Social System,* by Chalmers Johnson. 1964. 69 p. $1.50.

4. *Cuba: The Political Content of Adult Education,* by Richard R. Fagen. 1964. 77 p. $1.50.

5. *Americans in Black Africa up to 1865,* by Clarence C. Clendenen and Peter Duignan. 1964. 109 p. $1.50.

6. *Jordan River Partition,* by Georgiana G .Stevens. 1965. 91 p. $1.50.

7. *Territorial Claims in the Sino-Soviet Conflict: Documents and Analysis,* by Dennis J. Doolin. 77 p. $2.50.

8. *African Enterprise: The Nigerian Bread Industry,* by Peter Kilby. 1965. 112 p. Hard, $3.50; Paper, $2.50.

9. *The Israeli Communist Party and the Elections of the Fifth Knesset, 1961,* by Moshe M. Czudnowski and Jacob M. Landau. 1965. 101 p. $1.50.

10. *Soviet Local and Republic Elections,* by Max E. Mote. 1965. 123 p. $2.50.

11. *The Korean People's Democratic Republic,* by Glenn D. Paige. (Volume I of *Integration and Community Building Among the Fourteen Communist Party-States,* edited by Jan F. Triska.)

12. *The Mongolian People's Republic,* by Robert A. Rupen. (Volume II of *Integration and Community Building Among the Fourteen Communist Party-States,* edited by Jan F. Triska.)

13. *The Soviet Union in the World Communist System,* by Vernon V. Aspaturian. (Volume III of *Integration and Community Building Among the Fourteen Communist Party-States,* edited by Jan F. Triska.)

14. *The Chinese People's Republic,* by Dennis J. Doolin and Robert C. North. (Volume IV of *Integration and Community Building Among the Fourteen Communist Party-States,* edited by Jan F. Triska.)

Orders should be sent to: Publications Department, Hoover Institution, Stanford University, Stanford, California 94305.